revolve

revolve

A NEW WAY TO SEE WORSHIP

nelson searcy and jason hatley

WITH JENNIFER DYKES HENSON

BakerBooks

a division of Baker Publishing Group
Grand Rapids, Michigan

© 2011 by Nelson Searcy and Jason Hatley

Published by Baker Books
a division of Baker Publishing Group
P.O. Box 6287, Grand Rapids, MI 49516-6287
www.bakerbooks.com

Printed in the United States of America

Library of Congress Cataloging-in-Publication Data
Searcy, Nelson.
    Revolve : a new way to see worship / Nelson Searcy and Jason
Hatley with Jennifer Dykes Henson.
        p.   cm.
    ISBN 978-0-8010-1450-5 (pbk.)
    1. Worship. 2. Spiritual life—Christianity. I. Hatley, Jason.
II. Henson, Jennifer Dykes. III. Title.
BV10.3.S39 2011
248.3—dc23   2011024835

11   12   13   14   15   16   17   7   6   5   4   3   2   1

contents

acknowledgments

Nelson Searcy: I would like to dedicate this book to my two brothers, Michael Searcy and Danny Searcy. May our lives be an act of worship to our God and Lord. My utmost thanks to God for the opportunity to worship him now and for all eternity. I would also like to thank the co-contributors to this book: Jason Hatley and Jennifer Dykes Henson. I can't think of two better partners in writing or ministry. For their continued support and love, I must mention my wife, Kelley, and my son, Alexander. It's an honor to worship God with you daily. Beyond these, I must thank my close colleagues in life and ministry: Jimmy Britt, Kerrick Thomas, Scott Whitaker, Tommy Duke, Cristina

Fowler, Brendan Vinson, and Chad Allen and the excellent team at Baker Books.

Jason Hatley: Thanks to Nelson Searcy for the opportunity to write this book together and for the many years of partnership in leading people in worship. My thanks to Jennifer Dykes Henson for her tireless work to serve pastors and worship leaders. And finally to my wife, Karen, thank you for standing by my side (both onstage and off) for the last thirteen years.

Jennifer Dykes Henson: Thanks first of all to God for the opportunity and invitation to worship him every hour of every day. May we all discover the joy of living lives of continual worship! Thanks also to Nelson Searcy and Jason Hatley for inviting me into this incredible work that changes lives as it sheds light on God's truth.

introduction

Jon and Liz pull up to the church building a few minutes before the service is set to begin.

"Madison, come on. Stop reading and get out of the car. Johnny, don't forget your jacket," Liz says to her daughter and son in the backseat, as Jon cuts the engine but not the radio. Playoffs start this afternoon, and he wants to hear some of the predictions, even though he never agrees with the commentators.

Liz eyes him warily, so he turns the key the rest of the way and opens his car door. Truth be told, Jon hasn't been feeling that connected to God lately. At first, he felt engaged and alive every time he and Liz went to church, but recently he's been dry and sort of empty.

As the foursome moves through the front doors of the church, Madison and Johnny dart off to their respective classrooms with a quick wave. Jon and Liz head into the service, where Scott, the worship pastor, has already taken the stage. They slide into the end of a row, put their jackets on the chairs behind them, and start to . . . worship.

At least, Jon has always assumed that this is what worship is—this hour at church, the songs Scott leads them in. He moves his lips, singing inaudibly along with the others, but his heart feels far from worshipful. He begins thinking that maybe the style of music just doesn't suit him. *If they would just sing some more classic hymns, I could connect.* He glances over at Liz. Her hand is slightly raised, eyes closed, voice soaring.

Jon wonders what's wrong with him. This is his only opportunity during the week to worship God, and yet he gets absolutely nothing out of it. Something is wrong here, but he's not sure what.

Worship. Rarely has one little word been so powerful and yet so misunderstood. In fact, to prove the point, let's play a word association game. When you hear the word *worship*, what do you think of? (Check all that apply.)

___ a church service/worship service

___ a state of being

___ the songs you sing within a service

___ an activity that stokes your emotional fire

___ a responsibility

___ something that is led by a worship pastor

___ a daily activity

___ a privilege

___ something you do when things are going well for you

___ something you do when things are not going well for you

___ other: _____

The word—the entire concept—has become so muddled that many people have no idea what it means to worship God in truth.

Could true worship possibly be all of these things? Or maybe none of these descriptions is adequate. The word—the entire concept—has become so muddled that many people have no idea what it means to worship God in truth.

Now you know your starting point; you recognize your underlying view of worship. In the pages ahead, you'll discover a new way of seeing worship by digging into what it really is and how we are called to engage in it for our benefit and God's glory. Are you ready?

shifting perspectives

> When the subject is worship, the stakes are
> high—because worship is what God is all
> about.
>
> Louie Giglio

When I was in the seventh grade, I had a crush on a little dark-haired girl in my class. Her name was Samantha. Being the Casanova I was, I decided the best way to get Samantha to be my girlfriend was to challenge her to a bet. We had a big science test coming up, so I bet Samantha I would do better on the test than she would. The wager was a date with yours truly. If I won, she would have to go out with me. Genius, right? I thought so at the time. Mind you, I didn't really know what a date was, but I was ready to find out. In the unlikely event that I lost, she would subject me to public ridicule and humiliation. (That wasn't actually part of the bet, just a natural result of the situation. We're talking about the seventh grade, after all.)

Over the next week, I spent hours studying for that science test. I spent so much time in my room with my textbook that my mom called the teacher to ask if I was failing. The night before the test, I lay awake half the night, running through possible questions and answers in my head . . . and trying to decide what movie I was going to take Samantha to when this was all over. (I had asked my dad what you do on a date. "Go to the movies" was his answer, so I had also spent a good portion of the week scanning the Cineplex ads in the newspaper.) Anyway, when I finally fell asleep, I was ready. I knew I had this bet in the bag.

Well, God has always had a way of humbling me. Even after all the time and effort I put into studying for the test and closing the deal, I came up short. Samantha beat me by one measly question, and the much-publicized stakes became the source of my most memorable humiliation.

Believe me, the question she trumped me with is one I have never forgotten the answer to: who was the father of the scientific revolution? I confidently, albeit incorrectly, scribbled down "Copernicus." My fate was sealed. Samantha won, the shame commenced, and I went to see *Teen Wolf* by myself. Unfortunately for me, the father of the scientific revolution was not Copernicus but an obscure scientist who in the early 1600s began questioning some things he was seeing in the sky. The answer, of course, is Galileo. Which leads me to another story altogether.

Fresh Discoveries

Galileo Galilei (1564–1642) was an Italian physicist, astronomer, inventor, and philosopher who changed the way we understand the world around us. Thanks to his telescope—a new invention at the time—Galileo was the first to see other planets and stars at close range. As he began observing the workings of the solar system from this new vantage point—particularly the course of the moons of Jupiter—Galileo realized that the prevailing scientific view of his day was incorrect. He uncovered a truth that eventually went on to rock the modern way of thinking to its core.

15

The scientific establishment and general population in the 1600s subscribed to a geocentric view of the universe—the belief that the earth was the motionless center point and that everything else in our solar system revolved around it—a striking yet not surprising belief given that we, as humans, are so prone to assume that everything revolves around us. However, Galileo's observations pointed toward a new reality—one that led him to embrace the Copernican theory of a heliocentric universe. (I knew Copernicus factored in somewhere!) Heliocentric thought held that the sun, rather than the earth, was the center around which everything else revolved.

In 1610, Galileo published an account of his observations of the moons of Jupiter and what they meant for understanding the choreography of the universe. His findings were not well received, to say the least. As often happens when someone upsets the authority of accepted beliefs, Galileo met with bitter opposition from some philosophers and clerics. Eventually, his opponents denounced him to the Roman Inquisition. Although he was cleared of any immediate offense, the Catholic Church warned him to abandon his support for heliocentrism, calling it false and contrary to Scripture. Galileo promised to stand down . . . for the time being.

Fast-forward a couple of decades. Even after years of rebukes and threats from those in power, Galileo couldn't bring himself to remain silent about the reality of his discovery. In 1632, he outlined and defended his heliocentric views in his most famous work, *Dialogue Concerning the Two Chief World Systems*. The result? The Inquisition put him on trial, found him suspect of heresy, forced him to recant for fear of his life, and condemned him to spend the rest of his days under house arrest. It's not easy being a trailblazer. Becoming the eventual father of the scientific revolution came with a hefty price tag, but it was one Galileo was willing to pay. He couldn't deny the truth.

A New Paradigm

Though it took some time for the world to realize he was right, Galileo's discovery spurred a major paradigm shift about the galaxy we call home. Have you ever experienced a paradigm shift? A moment of clarity when you realize there's an entirely different way of seeing things than the way you've always seen them? A fundamental change in perspective that alters your approach to the world?

The concept of a paradigm shift first came on the scene in 1962 with Thomas Kuhn's work *The Structure of Scientific Revolutions*. Kuhn exposed the reality that nearly every noteworthy advancement in science is, at its core, a break with an old way of seeing the world—a break with an old paradigm. His revelation proved that to make strides toward any kind of advancement we must first recognize our current paradigms and then open ourselves up to the possibility of a new way of thinking. Galileo's discovery is a perfect example.

Perhaps the best way to illustrate the power of a paradigm shift is with an actual illustration. Take a look at the image below. What do you see?

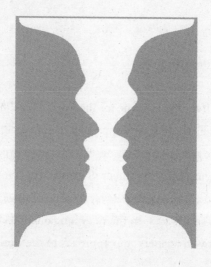

Depending on your perspective, you may see the profiles of two men staring each other down nose to nose, or you may see a beautiful vase. Which image do you see? Whichever one it is, another reality exists.

If you see the two faces, I have news for you: this is a picture of a decorative vase. But to see it, you have to shift your perspective. Here are some clues to help you see things a new way: the curve of the two men's necks creates the base of the vase. Their chins, lips, noses, eyes, and foreheads outline the detail and craftsmanship of the object. The space above the tops of their two heads is the vase's opening. Still don't see it? Try examining the image based on color. The vase is white on a black background, while the two faces are dark and set in front of a white background.

This little exercise underscores a monumental truth: we all tend to think we see things as they really are, but often that's just not the case. The scientific establishment in the 1600s was sure they were right in their beliefs about the solar system, but they couldn't have been more wrong. Their initial refusal to open themselves up to the reality of a heliocentric universe was a stubborn denial of measurable certainty and essential progress. Making the shift to a new reality took time, humility, and reason.

When we are able to open our minds to a new way of viewing the world, we give ourselves the opportunity to experience life-changing shifts. Galileo's study eventually sparked the scientific revolution—an all-encompassing paradigm shift based on absolute truth. Now we know,

---

We all tend to think we see things as they really are, but often that's just not the case.

---

without question, that everything revolves around the sun.

I would never want to be compared to any of Galileo's critics. I'm sure you wouldn't either. As progressive, educated people, we pride ourselves on being able to see the truth of situations and adjust our worldview accordingly, right? So what would you say if I told you that we are just as in need of a paradigm shift as the people who put Galileo under house arrest? What if, as a culture, we are blind to an overarching reality that directly affects our entire life? Even though it may strike you as hard to believe, we have a veil over our eyes too. We need a revolution of our own—a worship revolution.

the worship revolution

> All truths are easy to understand once they
> are discovered; the point is to discover
> them.
>
> Galileo Galilei

Scott closes the worship set with a prayer, and Jon and Liz sit down amid a rustle of papers and quick greetings. Jon runs his hand through his sandy blond hair and pushes a nagging guilt and longing into his gut.

"Good morning, everyone, and welcome," begins Pastor Tim. Jon hopes Tim will say something in his message that will light a spark and bring him back to where he used to be. He relaxes into his seat, ready to take in all he can.

Four Worship Myths

When it comes to worship, much of what we believe is as wrong as thinking that the sun revolves around the earth. Yet we persist in our false beliefs, because they are widely accepted and rarely challenged. Keeping your current view of worship in mind (as you acknowledged it in the introduction), let's take a look at four of the most common misconceptions we cart around:

1. Worship is about me.
2. Worship happens one day a week.
3. Worship is just a part of my life.
4. Worship is a religious activity.

These four misconcep-tions have become so in-grained in the psyche of today's church that I would call them *myths*. They have moved past being misinfor-mation and taken hold as false beliefs. They lead to an

Four Worship Myths

1. Worship is about me.
2. Worship happens one day a week.
3. Worship is just a part of my life.
4. Worship is a reli-gious activity.

anthropocentric view of worship—that is, the view that you are the center of your worship. Anthropocentric worship purports that worship is about you, your preferences, what

---

Worship is not about you.

---

you feel, what you experience, and what you can get. In the same way that some of the best scientific minds thought the universe was geocentric, many of today's most eager, thoughtful Christians think that this thing called worship re-volves around them. Are you ready for the paradigm-shifting truth that has the potential to launch an unprecedented worship revolution? Here it is:

Worship is not about you.

Worship is not meant to revolve around you any more than the sun is capable of revolving around the earth. No, just as God created the planets to revolve around the sun, he created worship to revolve around himself and his Son.

A Theocentric View of Worship

If you and I ever hope to worship God in a way that authentically connects us with his presence, we have to realize that worship is not about us. Worship is not about what we want and what we can get. Worship is about God, plain and simple. In the New Testament, Jesus's disciple John tells us, "All things were made by God and for God" (John 1:3, paraphrase). "All things" includes worship. Yet contemporary believers are given the subtle message that worship is by them and for them. Even when we don't mean to make it about ourselves, we often do, for two simple reasons: (1) by nature, we are inwardly focused; and (2) we've never been taught any differently. We are being impeded by the accepted thinking of our day.

Jon's experience is not unique. In fact, I would bet (my betting history aside) that you're able to relate to how Jon feels. Have you ever walked out of a church service feeling like you didn't get anything out of your time there? Have you ever wondered why you don't seem to be connecting with God during the week? Why the passion you once had seems to have dimmed?

As a pastor, I can't tell you how many times I've seen people come to church looking for something for them-

---

Until we understand that worship was created by God and for God, worship is never going to make sense.

---

selves only to leave feeling empty because they didn't receive what they thought they needed. Why weren't their longings fulfilled? They were operating out of the anthropocentric view of worship—they were making it all about them—and neglecting the reality that worship is a theocentric enterprise. Until we understand that worship was created by God and for God, worship is never going to make sense.

In the chapters ahead, we are going to uncover the truth about worship by debunking the four common myths mentioned above and digging into their corresponding, paradigm-shifting truths. I want to help you see that worship is a God-centered activity. It's not about your style, your preferences, your mood, or what you need. It's not about what you do in the hour you're at church. It's not about an attempt to be religious. Worship is about one thing and one thing only: bringing honor, glory, and pleasure to God. It's an activity that encompasses all of your life, not just part of your life. When you internalize the reality that worship is about offering your attention, your energy, your talent, and your focus to God—that it's about giving him the praise and adoration he deserves—you will begin to see your Father for who he is and begin to be able to worship him in truth.

When Galileo's contemporaries finally realized he was right, a revolution ensued and the seeds of current modern science were planted. Just imagine what could happen in the lives of worshipers today—in your life—if we accept the paradigm-shifting truth we have moved so far away from: that our worship is 100 percent about our God, in every way and all the time. I believe the seeds of the greatest worship revolution we've ever known would be planted, and it wouldn't be long before they would come forth in the form of connected, fulfilled, joyous worshipers around the world. Are you ready for a worship revolution?

tapping the heart of worship

> God's throne room allows no room for the
> proud. . . . He must increase and we must
> decrease. He must become greater and we
> must become less.
>
> Matt Redman

Matt Redman is a world-renowned worship leader
and respected songwriter who has written hundreds of worship songs that are sung in churches all over the

world. He is truly one of the great worship songwriters of our time. In the 1990s, Matt was based out of the Soul Survivor Church in Watford, England. As you might imagine, when a church's worship leader is internationally known for the songs he has written, the music in his own church is pretty phenomenal. Ironically, this led to a problem at Soul Survivor. Every weekend, the worship sets were off the charts. People would show up from around England to hear the worship team. While this may sound like a good problem to have, it wasn't. Things were out of whack.

A few years into Matt's personal success, he and the pastor at Soul Survivor noticed something: what had once been a time of authentic, heartfelt worship during their weekly services had slowly become a stale reflection of its former self. Now, the church had great musicians, amazing technology, and an incredible sound system. The people were singing extraordinary worship songs. In short, they had everything you would think would go into creating a great worship experience, but something was missing. In the buzz, excitement, and personal glory, truth had been lost. An imposter, me-centered worship had crept in and taken over so slowly that no one had noticed what was happening.

In his book, *The Unquenchable Worshipper*, Matt writes, "Where once people would enter into worship, no matter

what, we would now wait to
see what the band was like
first, how good the sound was
or whether we were into the
songs that had been chosen."[1]
People had come to expect

> And what greater ca-
> lamity can fall upon a
> nation than the loss
> of worship?
> Ralph Waldo Emerson

both an atmosphere that was pleasing to them and a high-level, engaging performance from the worship team. They would only enter into any kind of personal worship when and if these expectations were met. And even then, the worship was often inauthentic and incorrectly focused.

So Matt's pastor decided to take drastic action in hopes of fixing the problem. Late one Friday night, with the help of some fellow staff members, he snuck into the auditorium and removed the sound system and all the instruments. When Matt showed up on Sunday morning, everything was missing. There was no guitar, no keyboard, no speakers, and no worship team. On that Sunday morning, the congregation of Soul Survivor was not going to be able to worship in the way they had come to expect.

Imagine this scenario playing out in your church. What if you showed up for worship one Sunday morning and there was no music, no musicians or choir, no hymnals or video screens to provide you with the words to sing. Would you be able to worship God? Matt's pastor wanted to teach the congregation that worship is not for us but God. It's not about the songs we enjoy singing or a feeling we get but about bringing honor and happiness to him. As the psalmist writes, "Not to us, O LORD, not to us, but to your name goes all the glory for your unfailing love and faithfulness" (115:1 NLT).

In Matt's church, the music and the worshipers had become the revolving point of worship, usurping God's central position. Worship was no longer about bringing glory to God; it was about achieving an experience. Ultimately, this congregation had become focused on bringing glory to itself.

As we touched on in the last chapter, we all have a tendency to think that worship is about us. This false belief is rooted in the first myth people buy into about worship:

Myth #1: Worship is about me.

You and I were created to worship, but we were not created to worship ourselves. The danger of making worship about our own feelings and desires is that, by doing so, we are making ourselves the center point of our worship. Even though we are professing to worship God, we are really worshiping our own interests. No wonder this kind of worship leads to emptiness. In reality, worship is not about you but God.

Paradigm Shift #1: Worship is not about me but God.

When we make worship about us, we fall into the trap of judging our worship based on our emotions. We think that if we feel warm, tingly, and connected to God, then we've worshiped; if we don't, well, something's wrong. But this thinking stems from the false belief that worship is about us.

You and I were created and exist to bring pleasure to God. In fact, that's the definition of worship: bringing pleasure to God. The Bible tells us, "You are worthy, O Lord our God, to receive glory and honor and power. For you created everything, and it is for your pleasure that they exist and were created" (Rev. 4:11).

When you walk into a worship service, if the people who lead worship have done their jobs, the details of that service have not been put together for your entertainment. Rather, everything that goes into creating a powerful worship service should be geared toward the singular goal of helping you get outside of yourself and focus on the holiness, righteousness, and goodness of God—to help you bring pleasure to him. When things are as they should be, the worship team, the artistic elements, and the message draw your attention away from your own concerns and gratification and toward the inescapable awe of your Creator.

"More Than a Feeling"

When Boston sang "More Than a Feeling" back in 1976, they weren't talking about worship. Still, the truth applies. When we make worship about us—when we set ourselves up as the revolving point around which worship should spin—we are, ultimately, looking for a feeling. We rely on our emotions to tell us when we have connected with God. But worship is not always a warm and fuzzy feeling. As I'm sure you've experienced as well, there are days when my quiet time or my time at church leaves me thinking, *I really didn't get a lot out of that.* But worship is not about me. Worship does not exist for my benefit. It's not about my pleasure but God's pleasure.

Of course, God wants us to sense his presence, but he is much more concerned that we worship him in truth. As Rick Warren writes, "Yes, he wants you to sense his presence, but he's more concerned that you trust him than that you feel him. Faith, not feelings, pleases God."[2] Feelings are a by-product. If we measure the depth of our worship solely in terms of how we feel, we've missed the boat. In fact, I would argue that our worship should be even more treasured

> Faith, not feelings, pleases God.
> Rick Warren

when we don't feel it. In those times, we know we have worshiped God because he is worthy rather than out of a self-seeking heart. As A. W. Tozer says in his great work *The Purpose of Man*:

> Worship is not confined to emotion and feelings, but is an inward attitude and a state of mind subject to degrees of perfection and intensity. It is not possible to always worship with the same degree of wonder and love as at other times, but wonder and love always has to be there.[3]

If you approach worship with the attitude, "God, what do you have for me?" you're always going to walk away empty. Instead, shift your perspective into alignment with

---

If you approach worship with the attitude, "God, what do you have for me?" you're always going to walk away empty.

God's truth by asking, "God, how can I give myself to you? How can I give you praise? How can I give you glory? How can I give you the worth you deserve?" Only then will you walk away from your time of worship deeply satisfied.

The Heart of Worship

So what happened at Matt's church? Slowly but surely people began to rediscover the heart of worship. They started to realize that worship wasn't about the songs they were singing but about the God they served. In *The Unquenchable Worshipper*, Matt goes on to say, "After a while the band and sound system returned, but this time things were different. The songs of our hearts had caught up with the songs of our lips."[4]

Matt discovered that God was revolutionizing his understanding of worship as a theocentric endeavor. After this experience, he wrote a song that encapsulates the truth that worship is not about us but God. This song, "The Heart of Worship," has become one of the most well-known and well-loved worship songs of an entire generation. The chorus speaks to the revolutionary paradigm shift of authentic worship: "I'm coming back to the heart of worship, and it's all about you, Jesus." As we internalize this truth, we'll finally be able to come back to the heart of worship ourselves. Remember, worship is not about you and me; it's all about him.

At the end of this and future chapters, we have included a section called "Revolve Thoughts." The intention of these sections is to go deeper on a specific issue related to worship.

Revolve Thoughts

Why Clapping Matters

In many churches, clapping is a natural part of the service. In others, not so much. If clapping is not a part of your church culture, that's okay. But if it's something you are considering or do from time to time, take a look at how clapping can help you worship.

1. Many people are kinetic learners. Clapping draws kinetically minded people into worship more than just standing and singing.

2. After wrestling with the kids all morning, busting out the door ten minutes late, and driving to church in the rain, it can be difficult to dive right into worship as soon as you walk through the church doors. Something as simple as clapping can help you shake off the morning's distractions.

3. Clapping leads to engaging. Engaging leads to singing. And singing leads to worshiping.

4. If you serve on the worship team, remember that congregation members will take their cues from you. In fact, I've found that they will give back about 10 percent of what you give them. That means if you want to kick-start the service with some high energy praise, you will have to lead in a bigger way than you think is comfortable. If you sing from the congregation, help your worship leaders out by following their lead. You will be worshiping in no time.

5. When you clap after a song, you're extending the moment of worship, not giving the worship leader a big ego. So go ahead and clap if the moment feels right.

monte carlos
and mundane moments

Without worship, we go about miserable.

A. W. Tozer

Monday, 6:00 a.m. "Rain today throughout the region and a high of . . ." blares Jon's alarm clock radio. He reaches over and smacks the snooze button, but he's wide awake. Staring at the ceiling, Jon is already chasing his thoughts. Thought #1: *The Packers won their playoff* *game yesterday, so there'll be a celebration lunch in the office today.* Thought #2: *I can't forget about the meeting with Kevin this afternoon.* Thought #3: *What Pastor Tim said yesterday in his message was right on time. Maybe I am too self-focused. Maybe that's why I've been so irritable lately.*

The radio screeches again. Jon reaches over and rouses Liz, then jumps out of bed and heads toward the kitchen to start the coffeemaker. As he's waiting for the caffeine to brew, he sees the program from yesterday's service lying on the kitchen counter. He picks it up and starts scanning through some of his notes.

Okay, so worship is not about me. I get that. I think my view of God has been too small. Carrying the notes back to the coffeemaker with him, Jon pulls out a mug and pours himself a strong dose. *But what about Tim's next point? Worship is not just for Sundays but every day. How can I worship if I'm not at a worship service? It's not like I can worship God at work. Not sure I get that one.*

Jon hears Liz coming down the steps. He tosses the program and notes aside and heads toward the front door to get the paper. When he steps out into the morning chill, he smells the faint aroma of a chimney a few houses down. His neighbor across the street backs out of the driveway and pulls away with a wave. Jon breathes in the cool, early morning air and senses a sort of awe, a kind of thankfulness.

He steps back inside, sets the paper on a side table, and heads upstairs to wake up Johnny and Madison.

Have you ever noticed that what you do every day carries more power than what you do a couple of times per week, once a week, or monthly? Say you want to start reading more. If you decide to read for thirty minutes every morning before your day gets started, you have set up a solid routine for yourself—you have a daily commitment to abide by. However, if you decide to read three or four mornings per week, your commitment will inevitably wane. You will spend a lot of time debating with yourself over which days to read. If you wake up on Tuesday morning feeling tired, you have the leeway to think, "Oh well, I'll just let this be a day off," and sleep in a little. But we all know how that goes. When you wake up tired on Wednesday morning too, well . . . you may end up falling short of your commitment. What we do every day becomes a habit. What we do periodically has a much harder time taking root.

When it comes to worship, the second major myth we buy into is that worship is something that happens on the one day each week we go to church.

Myth #2: Worship happens one day a week.

The truth is that, like most activities integral to our well-being, worship was created to be an everyday occurrence. The next paradigm shift we need to make in our understanding of worship is that worship is not just for Sunday but every day.

Paradigm Shift #2: Worship is not just for Sunday but every day.

The early church understood that worship was an everyday activity. King David famously said, "I will praise the LORD at *all times*. I will *constantly* speak his praises" (Ps. 34:1 NLT, emphasis added). Part of the reason we have moved away from constant worship and praise is that we have turned church into something we go to, and we have turned the idea of worship into something that happens at church. As a result, we have perpetuated the idea that God lives in the church building and that we worship him on Sundays—if the worship songs tickle our fancy. Harsh? Maybe, but all too true.

> If we are going to worship in Spirit, we must develop a spirit of worship.
>
> Michael Catt

This mind-set is exacerbated by the fact that we live in a spectator society. We go to movies, plays, and baseball games. We sit in front of our television sets expecting to be entertained. This modern expectation has crept into the church as well. We walk through the doors of the church building and are handed a program. Then we take a seat facing a stage or a podium and wait for the show to begin. But as author Louie Giglio writes in his work on praise and worship, *The Air I Breathe,* "Worship isn't something you attend, like a movie or a concert. Worship is something you enter into with all your might. Worship is a participation sport in a spectator culture."[5]

Contrary to popular belief, worship is not something that takes place only in a church service. In fact, it has little to do with actual planned services. While our participation on Sunday mornings is a requirement of a thriving

> *Worship is an all-the-time, consistent endeavor, just as David modeled.*

faith, worship neither begins nor ends at church. Rather, worship is an activity God calls us to engage in each and every day—when we wake up in the mornings, when we hear our children laugh, when we feel overwhelmed at work, when we embrace our spouse, when we see a sunset, when money is tight, when we enjoy a great meal, when

41

we see a long-lost friend, when our family members are driving us crazy, when we breathe in the spring breeze . . . you get the picture. Worship is an all-the-time, consistent endeavor, just as David modeled. Worship is not just for Sunday but every day.

This Is the Day

When I was growing up, my parents made sure that my brother and I were in church every Sunday (as their parents had done with them). Unlike a lot of kids, I actually enjoyed going to church. I would wake up on Sunday mornings and put on my dressiest clothes, which for most of my adolescent years included a clip-on tie. My mom, dad, brother, and I would hop in my mom's 1976 Monte Carlo and make the short drive to church. When the service was over, we would pile back into the car and head home. As soon as we got through the front door, I would bolt to my room, pull off the clip-on tie, and toss it on a shelf—along with my Bible—until the next Sunday. Then my parents, brother, and I would spend the afternoon lazing around the house, watching whatever sport happened to be in season.

I didn't think about God much during the week. Thoughts of church and worship were crowded out of my mind by thoughts of math tests and baseball cards. It wasn't until years later, when I began my own personal relationship with God, that I began to understand that he doesn't live just in the church building. I realized that I can pray, read my Bible, and sing songs of worship Monday through Saturday too and that God is okay with that—in fact, it is his desire for me. God wants more of me than just one hour of my time each week. He wants me to engage with him every day.

Have you ever found yourself caught in this Sunday trap? Let me ask it this way: have you ever been guilty of leaving church, chucking your Bible onto the backseat of the car, and not thinking about worship again until six days have come and gone? If so, you aren't alone. Churches are full of Christians who operate the same way. Now, I'm not saying they aren't earnestly interested in seeking God—they simply don't understand what that entails. They look forward to worship on Sunday because they see it as the only day of the week when they will have an opportunity to encounter God. I call this mind-set the "All-You-Can-Eat-Buffet Syndrome."

We all love all-you-can-eat buffets, right? We get to gorge ourselves and feel frugal at the same time. You know how it works. You pile your plate so full that you aren't sure you can walk back to the table without something falling off. Then you stuff yourself silly. When you finish eating, you say, "Wow, what a great meal. I don't think I need to eat again for an entire week." But you know that won't work. No matter how much food you eat during one sitting, by the time five or six hours or so go by, you are going to be hungry again. You are going to need fresh nourishment for your grumbling stomach.

Why is it, then, that so many of us think we can get our fill of God on Sunday and then put worship on the shelf until the next Sunday? As long as we treat God like a buffet, we are going to live an unsatisfied life of faith. As an aside, this is why some people have a hard time finding a church home. They are looking for a church that will feed them enough in one sitting to last throughout the week. Whenever a church is unable to do that, they decide to give another one a shot, with the same expectations. Time and time again, they become frustrated, never realizing that they are asking a church to do their job for them.

No church can feed you enough on Sunday to sustain you until the next service. Part of growing as a follower of Christ is learning to cook for yourself during the week. You have a responsibility to seek your own nourishment through Bible study, prayer, sharing your faith, and being involved in activities and community groups with other believers.

The "All-You-Can-Eat-Buffet Syndrome" is a by-product of the myth that worship is something that happens only on Sunday. When you buy into this myth, you are missing the point of worship. If the definition of worship is to bring pleasure to God, why in the world would it be confined to one day each week? Stop starving yourself and begin indulging in true, everyday worship. God takes delight in us, and he wants us to take delight in him as well—every day.

The Habit of Worship

The key to making worship a part of our daily life is to get into the habit of worshiping God whenever we are in his presence. So the question becomes, when are we in his presence? We are in God's presence every moment of our lives:

> You know when I sit down or stand up.
> You know my thoughts even when I'm far
> away.

You see me when I travel
    and when I rest at home.
    You know everything I do.
You know what I am going to say
    even before I say it, LORD.
You go before me and follow me.
    You place your hand of blessing on my head.
Such knowledge is too wonderful for me,
    too great for me to understand!
I can never escape from your Spirit!
    I can never get away from your presence!
If I go up to heaven, you are there;
    if I go down to the grave, you are there.
If I ride the wings of the morning,
    if I dwell by the farthest oceans,
even there your hand will guide me,
    and your strength will support me.
I could ask the darkness to hide me
    and the light around me to become night—
but even in darkness I cannot hide from you.
    To you the night shines as bright as day.
    Darkness and light are the same to you. (Ps.
    139:2–12 NLT)

When we become aware that the all-knowing presence of God permeates our minute-by-minute reality, we will be better able to worship him every day. In his work on

this topic, *Praise Habit*, David
Crowder writes, "When good
is found and we embrace it with
abandon, we embrace the Giver
of it." His premise is that when
you open your eyes to the blessings around you and recognize

> When I admire the won-
> der of a sunset or the
> beauty of the moon, my
> soul expands in wor-
> ship of the Creator.
>
> Mahatma Gandhi

that everything good comes from God (James 1:17), you
can find him everywhere. He continues, "Yes, in church on
Sunday at 9:00 a.m., but also in the seemingly mundane. In
traffic on Tuesday at 5:15 p.m. In a parent-teacher meeting.
In the colors of a sunset. On the other end of a tragic phone
call. Every second is an opportunity for praise. There is a
choosing to be made."[6]

Crowder's last point is an important one. There is a
choosing to be made. The impetus is on you and me to
make the choice to worship God every day of the week, in
every circumstance we face. Worship is not always going to
be our default—especially when things in life aren't going
as well as we would like. But by discovering how to practice
worship regularly, we can raise our level of continual praise.

To get started, let me suggest an exercise: take the next
ten days and intentionally practice worshiping. Here are
three steps to help you work a worship habit into your
daily life:

1. *Give God your first fifteen.* Commit to spending the first fifteen minutes of your day with God. As soon as you roll out of bed, open your Bible and read a few passages. Spend a few minutes in prayer. If you don't know what to read, start with the book of Psalms. It's full of ideas about how you can live a life of worship every day. (For a detailed Bible reading plan, visit www.RevolveBook.com.)

2. *Say breath prayers.* Throughout your day, pray quick breath prayers. They may be something as simple as, "God, thank you for my job" or "God, help me deal with this situation with my children." Frequent, simple prayers remind us both to trust God and to thank him for what he is doing in our lives.

3. *Pray at bedtime.* Whether you said your bedtime prayers as a child or not, it's time to pick up the practice. Before you go to sleep, take a few minutes to reflect on your day and acknowledge the ways God has blessed you. Thank him for those blessings. Even if you had a difficult day, learning how to acknowledge God's continual presence and thank him in every situation is key to living a life of worship. Situations change for better or for worse, but God's worth never changes.

Revolve Thoughts

What to do if you arrive early for Sunday worship:

1. Pray that everyone who attends the service will have an open heart.
2. Pray for God to open your heart.
3. Pray for the pastor and worship pastor.
4. Prepare your offering.[7]

What to do if you arrive late for Sunday worship:

1. Take a moment before you get out of the car to focus your mind on God. You are already late. An extra fifteen seconds won't matter, and the payoff will be great.
2. Enter quietly and take a seat discreetly.
3. Pray for the service as you enter.
4. No matter what is happening when you walk in, take a moment to focus yourself on the environment and ask God to allow you to truly worship.
5. Engage the rest of the worship service fully.

What to do during the greet time:

Greeting others is awkward for some—including me; I'm pretty introverted. Hopefully, your church keeps the greet time short. As a general rule, I counsel churches to do a greet time so the extroverts feel welcome but to keep it short so the introverts don't feel unwelcome. Here are a few tips to help you get through it—and maybe even enjoy it:

1. Wear a big smile as you greet people.
2. Say your name first.
3. Make it a point to speak to someone you don't know rather than just saying hello to those you do know.
4. Be one of the first to sit down. It will help bring the greet time to a nice, neat end.

In his letter to the Romans, the apostle Paul writes:

> So here's what I want you to do, God helping you: Take
> your everyday, ordinary life—your sleeping, eating,
> going-to-work, and walking-around life—and place it
> before God as an offering. Embracing what God does for
> you is the best thing you can do for him. Don't become so
> well-adjusted to your culture that you fit into it without
> even thinking. Instead, fix your attention on God. You'll
> be changed from the inside out. (Rom. 12:1–2 Message)

Paul's words provide the secret to living a life of worship
every day. When we take our "everyday, ordinary life" and
lay the details of it before God, we will move from being
once-a-week worshipers to being daily worshipers. And,
as Paul says, we will be changed from the inside out. In
other words, we will experience our own personal worship revolution.

finding your center

> The more we let God take over, the more
> truly ourselves we become—because he
> made us.
>
> C. S. Lewis

Our spiritual health and our physical health have a lot in common. Have you ever set out to lose a little weight? Whether you were successful or not, I'm sure you learned early on that diets don't work. Sure, they may help you drop a few pounds in the short term, but as soon as you go off the diet, you gain the weight back. As a result, millions of people yo-yo back and forth between numbers on the scale as they dive into one diet after another. Why don't these diets do the trick? Because they are nothing but limited-view solutions for something that is a lifestyle issue.

Our bodies will never achieve and maintain the weight—not to mention the level of health—God intends

---

Worship that truly honors God, as it prompts us into his will for our lives, is worship that has moved from being an activity to a lifestyle.

---

unless we make mindful eating and exercise a lifestyle. We can't just pay attention to our bodies every once in a while when things start feeling out of whack. No, we have to commit to a lifestyle of health if we ever hope to reach our potential.

The same goes for worship. Worship that is reserved for a weekend service, or for when we are struck by a random spirit of thankfulness, is limited-view worship. Worship that truly honors God, as it prompts us into his will for our lives, is worship that has moved from being an activity to a lifestyle.

Unfortunately, too many of us approach worship the same way we approach our health. We think it is just one piece of the overall pie—something to be addressed at certain times and for brief durations. In short, we buy into the third major myth of modern worship.

Myth #3: Worship is just a part of my life.

With worship, as with our health, this simply isn't true. If you spend your life trying fad diets and exercising only sporadically, your health is going to suffer. And without your health, your entire life and purpose are in jeopardy. Physical health is not a stand-alone enterprise. In the same way, if you confine worship to just a part of your life, your overall relationship with God will suffer. Every other area of your life will suffer. You will become frustrated and disconnected. Worship is not a stand-alone enterprise. It is meant to saturate, bolster, and shape every area of your life.

Paradigm Shift #3: Worship is not a part of my life but all of my life.

Authentic worship is the natural response to a proper understanding of God—the kind of worship that isn't focused on me and doesn't just happen at certain times.

Worship, in its truest form, is the offering of our entire life up to God. It's a moment-by-moment, day-by-day activity that encompasses who we are. In fact, worship that is anything other than a lifestyle is something of a new invention. In biblical times, people were great at praising God continually—at home, in battle, at parties, and in jail. Worship infused every area of life, as is God's desire. Without a consistent lifestyle of worship, we yo-yo back and forth in pursuit of the peace and the potential God has planned for us.

Wired for Worship

God isn't playing tricks on us. He wouldn't demand our continual worship if he didn't wire us to be continual worshipers. He did. All it takes is a quick look around to see that humans were created to worship. Here are a few examples of the way our innate need to worship shows up:

- **Sports teams.** We've all known sports fanatics who live and die by their team's record. There's nothing wrong with being a fan, but when people begin staking their emotions and even their identity on a sports team, things have gotten out of balance. Why does this happen? We are wired to worship. We have a deep need to be called up into something bigger than ourselves.

- **Celebrities.** You could walk into a hundred different concert venues tonight and see people worshiping. Thanks to our wiring, we elevate celebrities—musicians and actors, primarily—to God-like status and then worship at the altar of their art. When it comes to concerts, our outward signs of worship even look like the worship that's described in the Bible. We raise our hands, lift our voices, cry out, and dance.

- **The almighty dollar.** Anyone who thinks the Western world doesn't worship money has been checked out of modern life since the dawn of the Industrial Revolution. Countless people wake up every morning and go to sleep every night with their thoughts centered on money—how much they have, how much they need, how they can get more, and what they can buy when they get more. We make decisions based on money, fill our conversations with money, and enter into relationships with money in mind. As Mark Twain famously said, "Some men worship rank, some worship heroes, some worship power, some worship God, and over these ideals they dispute and cannot unite—but they all worship money."[8]

Everyone worships something. *You* worship something. You can't help it; you were created to worship. If you choose not to place God in the central position of worship in your life, you will fill the space with something else. You may not mean to; it's just who you are.

Identifying the Focal Point

Since God created you, and you can't help but worship, it makes sense that your worship is intended for God's glory. In fact, the goal of worship is to put God in his rightful position as the focal point of your life. Just like the sun is the focal point for the earth's rotation, every individual needs a focal point around which to revolve. God's plan is that he would be our center, but that doesn't always happen. Even thoughtful Christians often revolve around something or someone else without realizing what they are doing.

But here's the bottom line: no one is walking around without a focal point in place. Every person you know has something at the center of his or her life. Whether it's money, career, family, a spouse, pleasure, or something else, every soul is revolving around a specific point, whether intentionally chosen or by default.

As we dig a little deeper, we uncover a startling truth: you worship whatever you put at the center of your life. If

---

The goal of worship is to put God in his rightful position as the focal point of your life.

---

you have placed luxurious living in that central spot, you worship a lush lifestyle. If you have placed your children in that position, you worship your children. If you have placed climbing the corporate ladder at the focal point, you worship advancement. How many times have you known a teenager to fall in love and suddenly seem to worship the object of her affection? Her beau has become her focal point.

You can't help but worship what you center your life around. If you talk to someone who says he doesn't worship anything, he is simply blind to this truth. He worships something; he can't help it. If he doesn't know what he's worshiping, he is probably worshiping himself—a common occurrence in our me-centric culture.

Now, don't misunderstand me. Placing great importance on your career or your children or your spouse isn't a bad thing. Of course, you want to provide well for your family; you want to love the people around you the best you can. It's not innately negative to want to climb the corporate ladder and garner success. None of these things is a problem—when they are given the right priority in your life. While admirable in and of themselves, family, career, and other things of that nature were not designed to be at the center of your life. *You* weren't designed to be at the center of your life. You are not eternal; your family is not eternal; money is not eternal; only God is eternal.

The solid focal point of our life has to be something bigger than we are, something that is truly worthy of our worship. Deep down, we all know this is true, which is why we are so quick to become involved in causes larger than ourselves. We are drawn into stories, missions, and endeavors that touch a nerve of truth and make us feel like we are connected to a bigger picture. But the reality is that nothing we can experience on this earth will ultimately fulfill the God-shaped core of our lives. Only God is big enough for our worship. True worship involves putting him in his rightful position at the center of our life and allowing him to permeate our everyday being.

Oh, one other thing: whatever you worship is what you become. If you put yourself on the throne of your life, you are going to become selfish. If you worship money, you will become materialistic. This is a natural cause and effect. So we need to worship something that's going to draw the best out of us and form us into what we were created to be—worshipers of God. When we make God our focal point, we are drawn into him. We fall in love with him. We become like him and open ourselves to the reality of who we are meant to be.

> The instinct to worship is hardly less strong than the instinct to eat.
>
> Dorothy Thompson

It's time to ask yourself a difficult question: what's at the center of your life? What have you made your focus? What are you spending your days revolving around? How do you know? Easy. Just take a long, hard look at where you spend your energy, time, and money. If you were to show me your checkbook and your calendar, I would have a pretty good idea of what you worship. Whatever you put your time and money into—not what you give lip service to—is what you worship. Your heart may want to tell a different story, but your time and money don't lie. Take a step back and consider the trail of hours and dollar bills you leave in your wake. What are they geared toward? Is it

59

pleasure? Is it food? Is it toys to please your kids? Whatever it is, that's what you most value; that's what's at the center of your life. That's what you worship.

Planned for God's Pleasure

You and I were planned for God's pleasure, and he wants us to take pleasure in him. If you're married, do you remember when you first fell in love with your spouse? When I fell in love with my wife, I was completely focused on her. I constantly thought about how I could make her happy and what I could do to prove my love to her. She was the first thing on my mind when I woke up in the morning and the last thing on my mind at night. My new love for this woman spread throughout every fiber of my being. I couldn't get enough of her. I didn't want to be away from her. She was mine and I was hers, and that's all that mattered in the world. Anyone who has ever truly fallen in love knows just what I mean.

Worship is all about falling in love with God—entering into a relationship in which you can't get enough of him. You think of him constantly and want to do the things that bring him pleasure simply because you love him. You want to give him all of your life, everything about yourself. You want to be his forever, and you want him to be yours. Unfortunately, feelings like these don't always come naturally. They have to be encouraged and nourished. In fact, the Bible says we need to be reminded to turn our thoughts to God every hour, because if we don't, our mind begins to wander. Take a look at the psalmist's words: "From the rising of the sun to its setting the name of the LORD is to be praised" (113:3 NASB). When you read this verse, think of a sundial. As the sun moves across the sky, every single hour, the name of the Lord is to be praised.

I have to admit that I am often amazed by how long I can go without my thoughts turning to God. I am the pastor of a church with multiple locations and engaged in training other pastors—in short, my entire life is focused on ministry—and yet, more often than I like to admit, I can go for hours without thinking about God. Sometimes, in the middle of the day, I'll realize I haven't acknowledged God since that morning. I have learned that I need daily reminders, even hourly reminders, to turn my attention back to God.

As we discovered in the last chapter, choosing to start your day with God is a great way to center your focus. Saying breath prayers throughout the day is a powerful reminder of your dependence on your Creator. Here's another way to keep your conversation with God going all day. When you say your prayer in the morning, don't say amen. Don't put that finality on it. Just finish your prayer time with God and begin your day without signing off. Then, in a sense, everything you do during the day is a continuation of your time with him. Of course, this is always the reality, but not saying amen helps us make the mental shift into this truth. You'll also be more likely to pick the conversation back up as your day unfolds.

I've also known people who like to give themselves a solid hourly reminder to turn their attention to God by setting an alarm. If they work at a desk, they may set an hourly alarm on their computer to remind them to come before God for a few minutes. If they aren't near a computer, they may set the timer on their watch to go off every hour. Whatever the method, the point is to put a tool in place that will help them remember to turn their thoughts to God from the rising of the sun to the setting of the same.

What type of reminder would work for you? Why don't you try putting something in place? Set up a system that will remind you to engage with God on at least an hourly basis, to say to him, "God, I'm not going to let an hour go by without turning my attention to you, without acknowledging how worthy and glorious you are." As you do this, your thoughts will begin to turn to God more often without the little reminders. Worship will become a lifestyle. You will begin to speak to your Father with thanksgiving and love consistently. You will begin to make your relationship with him not just a part of your life but all of your life. That's true worship.

Revolve Thoughts

True worshipers:

- see worship as an act of *giving* rather than *receiving* (These worshipers focus on giving God their attention, time, treasure, and relationships. If they receive as well, that's great, but they always give.)
- bathe their worship in prayer, both privately and corporately
- celebrate the giving of tithes and offerings, because they know that God loves a cheerful giver (2 Cor. 9:7)
- intentionally avoid a critical mind-set
- are doers of the Word, not just hearers
- never dismiss something because it seems too shallow or too deep but consider everything from the perspective of "What does God want to teach me?"

debunking religion

> The great crisis of the churchgoer is that his
> action does not save him. He must base his
> faith on someone outside his control. He
> cannot make Christ redeem him, or manipu-
> late Christ into redeeming him. He can only
> trust Christ. And this is a frightening reality.
>
> Donald Miller

After Samantha won our little bet, it took a few weeks
for life to go back to normal, but eventually it did.
The years flew by, and before I knew it, I was a sophomore

in high school. Samantha was dating the president of the chess club, and I was knee-deep in writing computer-programming code. A couple of things are lodged in my memory from that year. First of all, I vividly recall driving from the DMV to my high school the morning I got my license. Second, I remember walking into my history class one day and the teacher passing out a textbook on the history of the world's religions. Since I had never thought much about religion, I was fascinated with the sheer number and diversity of belief systems: Buddhism, Hinduism, Islam, Judaism, Sikhism, and of course Christianity, to name a few. I spent hours poring over that textbook. I can still see the worn blue and gold cover.

Not until several years later, when I became a Christian, did I realize something shocking: Christianity shouldn't have been in that book at all. Why? Because Christianity is not a religion. Yes, you read that correctly. Christianity is not a religion. Surprised? Let me explain. Even though Christianity is often labeled a religion, it doesn't fit the traditional religious mold. Religion, by nature, is a human-centered enterprise. The vast majority of world religions are about people trying to work their way to God. In one form or another, they advocate following set rules and adhering to specific rituals in an attempt to garner acceptance and approval from a higher power. Comparatively,

Christianity is the antithesis of religion. Christian belief hinges on what God has done to show his love for us and secure our right standing with him rather than what we can do to earn them.

The problem is everyone thinks Christianity is a religion. I bet you have always thought so, right? Earnest Christians and unbelievers alike classify Christianity as a religion. This may not seem like a big deal at first glance. If we keep the definition of religion broad, calling it merely a belief in a higher power, Christian faith can make the cut. But religion goes much deeper than mere faith in a higher being. Even many agnostics have a belief in a higher power, but agnosticism certainly couldn't be thought of as a religion. At its core, religion is about work—work for justification, for favor, for a better life, for blessing, and the list goes on.

When Christianity is classified as a religion, the religious emphasis on ritual, self-effort, and works seeps into our understanding of the faith—including our understanding of worship—and creates confusion. Many unassuming Christians, then, begin to see worship as one of many religious activities under the umbrella of Christianity.

Myth #4: Worship is a religious activity.

But neither Christianity nor worship has anything to do with conventional religion. While religion is man centered,

Christianity is relationship centered. Rather than being about what we do to earn God's favor, it's about who we are in Jesus Christ. Worship is ultimately not about a religion but a relationship.

Paradigm Shift #4: Worship is not about a religion but a relationship.

Digesting this reality has the power to move us from *religious* worship to *authentic* worship. Religious worship stifles authentic worship. Since religion focuses on acts, religious worship presses worshipers into a perversion of the type of worship God intends. Worship becomes a game of "What can I do to get God to bless me?" We begin to think that if we sing the right way, or repeat the Apostles' Creed, or take communion every week that God will respond by giving us what we need.

Now, don't misunderstand me: there's nothing wrong with wanting to sing well for God, or repeating the Apostles' Creed, or taking communion regularly, when it's done with the right motivation. But when these things—or anything for that matter—become religious rituals that we perform in an attempt to win God's favor, we are going

> An authentic life is the most personal form of worship. Everyday life has become my prayer.
>
> Sarah Ban Breathnach

to miss authentic worship every time. In fact, God detests religious worship. Take a look at what he has to say about it in Isaiah:

> And so the LORD says, "These people say they are mine. They honor me with their lips, but their hearts are far from me. And their worship of me is nothing but man-made rules learned by rote." (29:13 NLT)

How is it that we are so easily persuaded into this kind of religious worship? Again, our Western culture is one of the culprits. We have been raised with a do-it-yourself mentality. As progressive, self-sufficient Westerners, we think in terms of cause and effect: what I do determines what I get. If we don't have what we need, we're told to pull ourselves up by our bootstraps and go after it harder. We think that if we control the variables, we can control the outcome. While this may be a great attitude to have in many other areas of life, it is not true with God. Author Fritz Ridenour sums up our tendency toward religious effort as an attempt at control.

> Christianity is more than a religion, because every religion has one basic characteristic. Its followers are trying to reach God, find God and please God through their own efforts. Religions reach up toward God. Christianity

is God reaching down to man. Christianity claims that men have not found God but that God has found them. To some this is a crushing blow. They prefer religious effort—dealing with God on their own terms. This puts them in control. They feel good about "being religious."[9]

Handing the responsibility for our salvation over to God can be threatening. If acceptance and atonement don't come as a result of how good we are, then how can we know for sure we are going to be accepted? In Christianity, there is only one action we have to take to win God's acceptance, and that is to choose a heartfelt relationship with Jesus over the rules and regulations of traditional religion. When we recognize the truth of Jesus's message, we have to give up our perceived ability to control God and, instead, hand ourselves over to his grace. Jesus himself tells us, "No one can come to the Father except through me" (John 14:6 NLT).

These words leave us no choice but to let go of the comfortable security of our religious routines and recognize that Jesus—and nothing else—is the source of our salvation. If you've been raised in an environment in which you've been taught to follow rules to earn God's favor and made to feel guilty when you didn't live up to certain standards, wrapping your mind around resting in a relationship with Christ may not be easy. But authentic worship is waiting on the other side.

My Story

I became a follower of Jesus a little differently, and a little later, than most people might expect. I actually asked Jesus to come into my life right around my eighteenth birthday. Until that point, I had been consumed with some other things—mainly, as I mentioned, computer programming. I actually started a computer business while I was in high school. By the time I hit seventeen, I was working on an engineering degree at North Carolina State University, while traveling and speaking at various conferences for young entrepreneurs.

At one of these conferences, I met a guy who had written a book I wanted to read, so I headed to a local bookstore to pick it up. While I was there, I noticed a book by Billy Graham called *Peace with God*. I bought Dr. Graham's book on a whim, thinking it was a history book about a guy I had heard a little about while growing up in North Carolina.

So in October of 1989, I was reading *Peace with God* and got to the page where Billy Graham offers an invitation of salvation to anyone reading the book who doesn't know Jesus. I prayed the prayer typed out for me there and then saw a toll-free number he suggested I call. I went back to my little apartment in Raleigh and called the number. The person on the other end suggested I do a few things: read my Bible, pray, get involved in a good church, and make my decision public through baptism.

After I gave my life to God, he put me on a new path. I ended up getting a bachelor's degree in religion and psychology at Gardner-Webb University and then a master's of divinity degree at Duke University, while pastoring a little church outside Charlotte. Eventually, I moved to Southern California to work with Rick Warren and the Purpose Driven Community. Then, in 2000, Kelley and I moved to Manhattan to start The Journey Church.

If you haven't already traded in the confines of religion or the dubious goal of "being a good person" for a relationship with Jesus, let me invite you to pray the same prayer I prayed that fall day in North Carolina:

Dear God, I open my heart to you and invite you into my life. I confess that I am a sinner. I ask that you would forgive me of all that I've done wrong. Thank you for sending your Son, Jesus, who died for me and who gives me the opportunity to know you. I want to be your follower. Thank you for accepting me. In Jesus' name I pray. Amen.

If you just started a right relationship with Jesus, congratulations and welcome! Make sure you go to www.Revolve Book.com for more information about the decision you just made and some guidance on the best next steps for you to take.

You Don't Bring Me Flowers Anymore

Being in a relationship with Jesus puts you in right standing with God—there's no other action you need to take to assure his approval and your salvation—but that doesn't mean you stop taking the right actions. Rather, your motivation changes. We instinctively understand the underlying truth here when it comes to our human relationships. When we are in a healthy relationship, we treat the other person with respect; we do things to please rather than hurt or offend our counterpart. We aren't trying to win approval anymore; we are simply acting out of the overflow of a good relationship. Right actions are the natural result of a right relationship. A heart to please is a by-product of a loving, in-tune bond.

Here's the tricky part: right actions, on their own, do not necessarily indicate or guarantee a right relationship.

It's possible to do all the right things for all the wrong reasons, as we've seen with religion. Religious thinking pur-

---

A right relationship should motivate you to do the right things—out of love, not obligation.

---

ports that if you do things the proper way, a relationship will follow. But as I'm sure you are beginning to realize, this reasoning is backward. Instead, a right relationship should motivate you to do the right things—out of love, not obligation.

Thursday, 4:00 p.m. Jon stares at his computer screen, but he can't concentrate. His mind is still consumed with the argument he and Liz had that morning. *How could she be so selfish? Doesn't she see how hard I've been working lately?* He has thought back through the miscues and miscommunications a million times today, but he just can't shake the anger. *Whatever. It'll pass. It always does.*

An hour later, walking to his car, Jon passes a florist's shop. *I guess I should buy her flowers. Isn't that what you're supposed to do after a fight?* Even though he's still not over what happened, he heads into the shop, grabs a medium-sized bouquet, and waits while the clerk runs his debit card. When Jon gets to the car, he tosses the flowers on the passenger seat and drives home.

Liz hears Jon pull up in the driveway and opens the front door, anxious to make amends. She sees the flowers in his hand and feels hopeful that he's ready to move on too. He walks through the door, pushing the flowers her way. "Here are your flowers," he says without meeting her eyes.

"Oh! Huh . . . Thanks?" Liz says as the flowers suddenly shift in her mind from being a beautiful peace offering to being a worthless gesture. She heads toward the kitchen to find a vase.

Jon performed the right action, but since the relationship was still wrong, the action lost its meaning. So it is with religious worship: right actions/wrong relationship. Authentic worship, on the other hand, flows directly out of a right relationship with God. If you want to sing loudly or raise your hands or take communion or kneel before God or say the doxology as an outpouring of your love, go for it. That's authentic worship. But doing those things while engaged in a wrong relationship with God is a sham; it's the height of empty religious ritual. Again, worship has nothing to do with religion and everything to do with a relationship. In *The Reason for God*, Timothy Keller describes the dichotomy as religion versus the gospel and underscores the magnitude of motivation:

> There is, then, a great gulf between the understanding that God accepts us because of our efforts and the understanding that God accepts us because of what Jesus has done. Religion operates on the principle "I obey—therefore I am accepted by God." But the operating principle of the gospel is "I am accepted by God through what Christ has done—therefore I obey." Two people living their lives on the basis of these two different principles may sit next to each other in a church pew. They both pray, give money generously, and are loyal and faithful to their family and church, trying to live decent lives. . . . The primary difference is that of motivation. In religion, we try to obey the divine standards out of fear. We believe that if we don't obey we are going to lose God's blessing in this world and in the next. In the gospel, the motivation is one of gratitude for the blessing we have already received because of Christ.[10]

To have any meaning at all, right actions must grow from the seedbed of a right relationship. When we are in a relationship with Jesus, the power and love of that bond naturally drive us toward doing the things that please God—not because we have to but because we want to. Worship is not about a religion but a relationship. Authentic worship is our heartfelt response to God's goodness and love. When, out of the overflow of our relationship with Jesus, we shift from wanting to please God for our own purposes to genuinely ascribing worth to him for who he is, we will become true worshipers.

something of value

If my mind is not engaged in my worship,
it is as though I worshipped not.

Confucius

If I were to invite you to a dinner party at my house, I bet you wouldn't show up empty-handed. You would probably stop on your way over to pick up a small token of appreciation. And while grateful, I wouldn't be particularly surprised by the gesture, because it's not un-usual for the invited party to bring the host a small gift. I would also guess that you would want this sign of thanks to be something of relative value—maybe a bouquet of flowers or a box of chocolates. You wouldn't show up and hand me a half-eaten candy bar; that wouldn't qualify as worthwhile. As we all do when we are invited to be a guest in someone's home and partake of their generosity, you would want to walk through the door with something of worth.

In the same way, when you have an important celebra-tion coming up—maybe your wedding anniversary or a friend's birthday—you go to great lengths to find the perfect gift. You want to give something of significance. You don't wrap up a tarnished piece of jewelry or some-thing out of your closet that you don't want anymore. Since the relationship is important to you, you work to honor it by presenting your spouse or your friend with something of value, right? The time and thought we put into these simple human exchanges say something about how we see the relationship. So with that idea in mind, consider this question: what do you bring to God when you approach him in worship? Are you intentional about bringing him something of value, or do you show up empty-handed?

Wise Worship

The three wise men were on to something. When they heard about Jesus's birth, these three kings from the East set out to find and worship him. But they didn't come empty-handed. Taking a cue from Old Testament worship, they brought valuable gifts with them to present to the newborn baby Jesus. Matthew 2:11–12 tells us:

> They entered the house and saw the child with his mother, Mary, and they bowed down and worshiped him. Then they opened their treasure chests and gave him gifts of gold, frankincense, and myrrh. (NLT)

While biblical scholars debate the symbolic meaning behind the gold, frankincense, and myrrh, one thing is certain: these were valuable gifts, intended specifically to be offered to Jesus in conjunction with their worship of him.

The idea of bringing something to worship, however, didn't originate with the Magi. They were simply carrying on what had been a common occurrence throughout the history of worship. In the Old Testament, people always brought something of value to God in worship. In fact, they were commanded to do so. Scriptural teaching provided specific directions for the kind of worship that was pleasing to God, and that worship included both required and voluntary offerings. While these offerings ranged from animals to incense, they were all tied to a single overarching purpose: to present something valuable to God in worship.

Some worship offerings were designed to earn the forgiveness of sins. Others were to express praise, thankfulness, and devotion to God. Grain offerings were common. With

> *It still pleases God when we intentionally participate in worship by bringing something of value to him.*

a grain offering, the worshiper would pour oil over his best flour and sprinkle the concoction with incense. Then he would take this offering to the priest, who would burn it on an altar. Scripture tells us that this type of offering was pleasing to the Lord (Lev. 2:1–2). We've all heard about the animal sacrifices of the Old Testament. While these had various meanings depending on the context, they were often peace offerings, symbolizing gratitude and fellowship with God.

As a result of Jesus's birth, death, and resurrection, our standing with God can be right and secure without these kinds of sacrifices. We no longer have to present God with animals, grains, and incense the way the Israelites did in the Old Testament. Nonetheless, it still pleases God when we intentionally participate in worship by bringing something of value to him.

What to Bring to Worship

Just as bringing a small token of appreciation to a dinner party is a sign of gratitude for the invitation, there are certain things you and I can bring to God in worship that express both our love for him and our desire to honor him. As Peter writes, "Through the mediation of Jesus Christ, you offer spiritual sacrifices that please God" (1 Pet. 2:5 NLT). So the question then becomes, what kind of "spiritual sacrifices" should we offer? What can you and I—given our modern mind-set and culture—bring to worship?

The prophet Isaiah was a messenger of God who lived an incredible life. In fact, God chose him to foretell that Jesus would be born of a virgin (Isa. 7:14). This and his other prophecies were key predictors of what was to come in the New Testament. By looking at one of the turning points in

Isaiah's life, we can gain some insight into the three main things God would have us bring to worship: ourselves, our abilities, and our friends and family.

> It was in the year King Uzziah died that I saw the Lord. He was sitting on a lofty throne, and the train of his robe filled the Temple. Attending him were mighty seraphim, each having six wings. With two wings they covered their faces, with two they covered their feet, and with two they flew. They were calling out to each other, "Holy, holy, holy is the LORD of Heaven's Armies! The whole earth is filled with his glory!" Their voices shook the Temple to its foundations, and the entire building was filled with smoke. Then I said, "It's all over! I am doomed, for I am a sinful man. I have filthy lips, and I live among a people with filthy lips. Yet I have seen the King, the LORD of Heaven's Armies." Then one of the seraphim flew to me with a burning coal he had taken from the altar with a pair of tongs. He touched my lips with it and said, "See, this coal has touched your lips. Now your guilt is removed, and your sins are forgiven." Then I heard the Lord asking, "Whom should I send as a messenger to this people? Who will go for us?" I said, "Here I am. Send me." (Isa. 6:1–8 NLT)

What, therefore, should you bring to worship?

Yourself. The thing God wants most from you is the thing that only you can give him: yourself. You must bring yourself to worship. As we've discussed, God wants your authentic worship. He wants your heartfelt affection. He's not the least bit interested in the trappings of religious duty; he wants you to be engaged with him with the right focus and motivation. A life fully surrendered to God in worship flows directly out of a close bond with him.

Once you know Jesus personally, you can deepen your relationship with him the same way you deepen all your relationships: get to know him better by spending time with him. One of the keys to a deep walk with God is to make an intentional decision to invest time and energy in your relationship with him. When you do, you are putting yourself in a place where you can truly experience his presence and his voice.

When Isaiah saw the Lord in the verses above, it was not the first time he had been in contact with God. In fact, throughout the course of the first five chapters of Isaiah's writing, we see that he and God had communed many times. Isaiah sought God out and got to know him more deeply over the course of his life. His ability to talk with and hear from God was the result of their deep relationship. The same truth applies to your connection to God. If you want to be able to really worship God, to experience him and to hear from him in your life, you have to cultivate the relationship. How? Here are three ways to get started:

1. *Spend time with God daily.* We've already discussed the importance of giving God the first fifteen minutes of your day (see chap. 4). Spending time with God before your day gets started is an ideal way to grow closer to him. As you read his Word and pray, listen for his still, small voice, and then go through your day worshiping him for who he is.

2. *Spend time with other Christians.* Two of the most significant ways God reveals himself to us is through his Word and through the people he puts around us. In addition to spending time with God and his Word daily, make sure you are involved in community with other like-minded believers. This may be through a small group or Sunday school class at your church. Whatever the format, find and nurture relationships with other Christians.

3. *Attend Sunday service.* Worshiping God and learning about him in a corporate environment are critical to your growth. There is no such thing as a lone-ranger Christian. Every one of us needs the larger church. That's why the Bible encourages us not to forsake gathering together with other believers in

an organized service (Heb. 10:25). If you aren't currently part of a church, visit www.RevolveBook.com for some resources to help you find a healthy church in your area.

Your abilities. Right before the old Yankee stadium was about to close its doors for good, I got a call from a friend with an offer I couldn't refuse. When I picked up the phone, my friend said, "Hey, man, I have two tickets to tonight's Yankees game. Want to go?" Did I want to go? I was ecstatic! My wife and I are huge Yankees fans. I jumped at the chance. My mind was already racing ahead to the matchup when my friend broke my train of thought with, "By the way, a business associate of mine gave me these tickets, so they are great seats!" My excitement doubled.

Fast-forward to the game. Every other time I had ever been to a game at Yankee Stadium, I had sat at least a couple of tiers up or out on the bleachers. Not this time. When we got to the game, we were shown to seats three rows behind first base. I could hardly contain myself. I had never seen the field from that perspective. Not to mention, these were unimaginable seats. They were padded and actually comfortable. There were celebrities down the row from us. A waiter came and asked us if we'd like to order peanuts and Cracker Jacks instead of having to stand in line. The game itself was incredibly exciting. It was almost a perfect night. Almost.

Sometime around the seventh-inning stretch, I asked myself a question that ended up spoiling the game for me. I asked myself, "How could this night be any better?" While I intended the question as rhetorical, an answer slapped me in the face. There was one thing that would have made that night ten times more thrilling and more fulfilling than it was: if I had been able to put on the pinstripes. What if I had been able to pick up a bat, step up to the plate, and hit one out of the park? What if I had made a diving grab and thrown someone out at first base? If I had been in the game, rather than just a spectator, that night would have been one of the greatest of my life.

Deciding to worship God with the abilities he has given you puts you in the middle of the game. Maybe you are great at bringing yourself to worship through your daily time with God, your relationship with other believers, and your involvement in church, but that's where it ends. When it comes to the specific gifts God has blessed you with, you hold back. You let other people step up and serve the church, the community, and the world. Rather than truly being a player in the only game that really matters, you are watching from the stands and missing out on significant, fulfilling experiences.

If you want your worship to go to the next level, offer your abilities to God. Pick up a bat, step up to the plate, and get in the game. God has given you specific talents and abilities that he wants you to use to build up his kingdom. There are certain activities you are uniquely gifted to perform. Maybe it's volunteering as a greeter at your church;

God has given you specific talents and abilities that he wants you to use to build up his kingdom.

---

maybe it's working with kids; maybe it's serving on a praise team; maybe it's volunteering in a homeless shelter in your community. Whatever it is, God wants you to use your abilities to worship him. Stop watching from the stands. Be willing to say to God, as Isaiah did, "Here I am" (Isa. 6:8). When you decide to step up and offer your skills in worship, you'll be amazed at how he can take your unique gifting and begin to use you in his diverse, magnificent work in your community and around the world.

Your friends and family. We've talked several times about falling in love. When you fall in love, you want to shout

it from the rooftops. You want everyone around you—
especially your friends and family—to know about the
incredible relationship you've found, right? The same is
true when you are passionately engaged in a daily walk
of worship with God. There is an undeniable connection
between your worship and your desire to tell your friends
and family about it. When worship is alive and real in your
life—when you are growing continually closer to God and
living your everyday life as an act of worship—you will have
a hard time not spreading the news to the people you love.

Evangelism exists to produce worshipers. God consid-
ers our friends and family to be valuable gifts that we can
entrust to him. Simply telling them about your relationship
with him is the first way you can bring them to worship.
Here are two more ways:

1. *Pray for them.* Bring your loved ones before God
   through prayer. Pray that they would see the power
   of your life of worship, that they would recognize
   their need to know God and find their center in
   him, and that they would be open to starting and/
   or growing a relationship with him.

2. *Invite them to church.* Most of us are timid when
   it comes to inviting someone to church, but we
   shouldn't be. Studies have shown that 55 percent

of people say they would attend church with a friend if they were invited. And that percentage goes up significantly if they are asked more than once. You have nothing to lose, and they have everything to gain. (Go to www.RevolveBook.com for a list of practical ways to share your faith with your friends and family.) Take your cue from Isaiah—don't be afraid to let God use you for his work in the lives of those around you.

Whom Shall I Send

At the end of our passage from Isaiah, the prophet writes, "Then I heard the LORD asking, 'Whom should I send as a messenger to this people? Who will go for us?' I said, 'Here I am. Send me'" (6:8 NLT).

When you and I realize that worship revolves around God, and internalize everything that entails, we are in a position to be true worshipers—to offer our everyday lives to him as a living sacrifice, to have him fill us with his love and presence. By choosing to bring something valuable to God in our worship—namely, ourselves, our abilities, and our friends and family—we are answering, with our lives,

God's question in the verse above. Only true, God-centered worshipers are able to say with Isaiah, "Here I am. Send me."

Revolve Thoughts

Five Ways to Worship without Music

1. *Pray*.
2. *Read your Bible*—and put what you read into practice.
3. *Tithe*. This is not just an Old Testament practice; it's a modern-day act of worship (2 Cor. 9:7).[11]
4. *Serve*. One of the best ways to take your worship to the next level is to serve in ministry at your church.
5. *Share your faith*. Want to draw close to God like never before? Pray for your friends who don't know him, invite them to church, and share your story.

conclusion

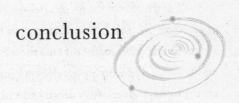

> It is only when men begin to worship that
> they begin to grow.
>
> Calvin Coolidge

Perhaps the reason Galileo's contemporaries had such a hard time believing his claim that the earth revolved around the sun is that they struggled, at their core, with the same issue we all struggle with—that is, thinking we are the center of our own universe. Despite the mounds of evidence to the contrary, we are all prone to think that we are the immovable force around which everything else revolves. You can admit it. It's part of our human condition. Of course, intellectually, we now understand what

Galileo proved about the sun's central position—just as we understand that we are not the end unto ourselves—but our lives and our focus tend to lead us back to the same mind-set that plagued his naysayers. In some deep part of ourselves that we may not like to acknowledge, we have a hard time admitting it's not about us.

Well, as they say in the medical world, an accurate diagnosis is half the cure. Acknowledging our tendency goes a long way. The other half of the cure for self-centered living and self-centered worship involves getting rid of the four myths we have successfully debunked and replacing them with these truths:

1. Worship is not about me but God.
2. Worship is not just for Sunday but every day.
3. Worship is not a part of my life but all of my life.
4. Worship is not about a religion but a relationship.

As we've seen throughout these pages, the way to experience a worship revolution in our lives is to acknowledge that we are not the center point. It's not about you. It's not about me. Worship is not about God revolving around our desires, our needs, our schedules, and our emotions. It's not about fitting God into a corner of our lives or trying to please him through religious tradition. Rather, it's all about God.

God is the immovable focal point, and everything in existence has been created to revolve around him. When we put him at the center of our worship, properly aligning ourselves with his truth, we will begin to experience the revolution we've caught a glimpse of here. We will step fully into the lives he has prepared for us, lives that are focused on him, lives that are greater than anything we could ask for or imagine (Eph. 3:20).

Sunday, 12:30 p.m. After catching up with a couple of friends, Jon and Liz head toward children's church to pick up Johnny and Madison. As they make their way down the hallway, Jon spots Pastor Tim through the crowd.

"Liz, can you get the kids? I think I'll go say hello to Tim," Jon says.

"Sure, we'll meet you at the car. Take your time." Liz smiles to herself as she watches Jon approach Pastor Tim. Over the last several weeks, she has seen a change in Jon. Of course, they've still had their moments—that fight last week being one of those moments—but who doesn't? Overall, Jon's perspective seems to be shifting on some things. He's been less focused on himself and has actually been more like the passionate man he was right after he became a Christian. Apparently, he has really been taking Tim's teaching on worship to heart. Liz turns the corner toward the classrooms as Jon approaches Tim and shakes his hand.

"Hey, Jon," Tim says. "Great to see you. How is everything?"

"Things are good, Tim," Jon answers. "Especially lately. I just wanted to let you know how . . . well, what you've been teaching lately has hit home. I had gotten sort of off base in my worship. It was all about this service on Sundays. Totally compartmentalized. But you've really helped me realize some things. I've been praying about this a lot lately,

---

Living a life of worship means living a life focused on pleasing an audience of one.

---

and God is steering me back toward himself. Just wanted to say I really appreciate it."

As Jon walks toward the car, he says a little prayer of thanks for the way God has intervened in his understanding of worship. When he opens the driver's side door, Johnny and Madison yell, "Daddy!" in perfect unison. Jon lets out a laugh at their enthusiasm and slides into the seat next to

Liz. She takes his hand as he pulls the car out of the parking lot and turns toward home.

Paul's words from his letter to the Romans are worth repeating here:

> So here's what I want you to do, God helping you: Take your everyday, ordinary life—your sleeping, eating, going-to-work, and walking-around life—and place it before God as an offering. Embracing what God does for you is the best thing you can do for him. Don't become so well-adjusted to your culture that you fit into it without even thinking. Instead, fix your attention on God. You'll be changed from the inside out. (12:1–2 Message)

Living your life as a true worshiper of God means offering yourself and everything you do to him. You don't live to please yourself or other people; you live to please the One who created you. You don't live to get what you can out of life; you live to give all you can to God and let him use you accordingly. In fact, to fully synthesize all we have discovered about worship, think about this final reality:

When God truly becomes your center—when you begin to revolve around him—your perspective shifts from the inside out and you realize that you are meant to live for an audience of one.

Let the paradigm-shifting truths you've discovered along this journey help you put God back at the center of your worship. Determine to live your life for an audience of one—the One who created you and takes pleasure in you. Then relish his greatness as he unleashes a worship revolution in your life.

notes

1. Matt Redman, *The Unquenchable Worshipper: Coming Back to the Heart of Worship* (Ventura, CA: Regal, 2001), 102.

2. Rick Warren, *The Purpose Driven Life: What on Earth Am I Here For?* (Grand Rapids: Zondervan, 2002), 110.

3. A. W. Tozer and James L. Snyder, *The Purpose of Man: Designed to Worship* (Ventura, CA: Regal, 2009), 107.

4. Redman, *Unquenchable Worshipper*, 103.

5. Louie Giglio, *The Air I Breathe* (Sisters, OR: Multnomah, 2003), 54.

6. David Crowder, *Praise Habit: Finding God in Sunsets and Sushi* (Colorado Springs: NavPress, 2004), 13.

7. For more information on giving, see Nelson Searcy, *The Generosity Ladder* (Grand Rapids: Baker, 2010).

8. "Money," *Mark Twain Quotations*, www.twainquotes.com/Money.html.

9. Fritz Ridenour, *How to Be a Christian without Being Religious* (Ventura, CA: Regal, 2002), 10.

10. Timothy J. Keller, *The Reason for God: Belief in an Age of Skepticism* (New York: Riverhead, 2009), 186.

11. For more information on giving that pleases God, see Searcy, *Generosity Ladder*.

Nelson Searcy is the lead pastor of The Journey Church. He served as the director of the Purpose Driven Community at Saddleback Church before starting The Journey Church in New York City in 2002. He and his two-thousand-member church appear routinely on lists such as the Fifty Most Influential Churches and the Twenty-five Most Innovative Leaders. The Journey is a multi-site church with locations across New York City and in Boca Raton, Florida. Searcy's newsletter for pastors and church leaders, *Church Leader Insights*, now reaches more than eighty thousand subscribers and continues to grow by hundreds each month.

Jason Hatley is the pastor of worship arts at The Journey Church and has been a worship leader since 1996. Jason was a part of The Journey's original launch team. He built from scratch The Journey's worship arts team, a group of over two hundred artists and technicians who develop and implement The Journey's creative and technical elements at the weekly Sunday service. Currently Jason serves as the pastor of worship arts at The Journey's newest location in Boca Raton, Florida. Jason is the founder of www.WorshipLeaderInsights.com. He has spoken at the Willow Creek Arts Conference, the Purpose Driven Worship Conference, and seminars across the country. He has a B.M. in sacred music performance from Appalachian State University.

Jennifer Dykes Henson is a freelance writer based in New York City. She has served as a writer/producer and ministry consultant to organizations across the East Coast. Prior to moving to New York, Jennifer worked with Dr. Charles Stanley as the manager of marketing communications for In Touch Ministries in Atlanta, Georgia. She is a member of The Journey Church.

WORSHIP AS ONE—UNITE MEMBERS AND LEADERS

For Worship Leaders

Engage, the church leaders' companion to *Revolve*, is a step-by-step, stress-free guide to planning worship services that allow for and foster true life change. Comprehensive in scope, *Engage* provides teaching pastors, worship leaders, and volunteers the tools they need to work together to develop and implement a worship planning system that improves communication, enhances creativity, and honors Jesus every week.

For Church Members

With *Revolve*, church members will see that when they approach worship with a "what can I get out of this" attitude, they're bound to be disappointed. However, worshiping God as a way of life not only honors God but also satisfied our souls. Built-in action steps at the end of each short chapter will give readers specific ideas about how to refocus their attention on God and live each day in an attitude of worship.

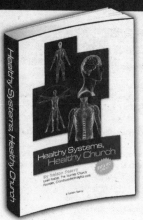